CEC Mini-Lib   P9-AOQ-984

**Exceptional
Children At Risk**

*B*orn Substance Exposed, Educationally Vulnerable

Lisbeth J. Vincent
Marie Kanne Poulsen
Carol K. Cole
Geneva Woodruff
Dan R. Griffith

Published by The Council for Exceptional Children

A Product of the ERIC Clearinghouse
on Handicapped and Gifted Children

Library of Congress Catalog Card Number 91-58307

ISBN 0-86586-212-5

A product of the ERIC / OSEP Special Project, the ERIC Clearinghouse on Handicapped and Gifted Children

Published in 1991 by The Council for Exceptional Children, 1920 Association Drive, Reston, Virginia 22091-1589
Stock No. P355

This publication was prepared with funding from the U.S. Department of Education, Office of Special Education Programs, contract no. RI88062007. Contractors undertaking such projects under government sponsorship are encouraged to express freely their judgment in professional and technical matters. Prior to publication the manuscript was submitted for critical review and determination of professional competence. This publication has met such standards. Points of view, however, do not necessarily represent the official view or opinions of either The Council for Exceptional Children or the Department of Education.

Printed in the United States of America
10   9   8   7   6   5   4   3   2

Contents

   The media have painted a dire picture of infants who were exposed to alcohol and other drugs in utero. This picture is not fully supported by research or clinical experience with these children: We do not know the incidence of prenatal exposure to alcohol and other drugs, nor do we know the long-term effects of such exposure.

   Many women who abuse alcohol and other drugs during pregnancy also experience other psychological, social, and medical events that can affect the health of their children. Thus, the risks of substance exposure are often compounded by other difficulties, such as inadequate housing, medical care, child care, and nutrition, that place these children at risk for developmental delays.

   A single agency usually cannot meet all of the needs of children and families dealing with the effects of exposure to alcohol and other drugs. A family-centered system of services is needed. There are a number of things educators can do to foster the growth of these children, including understanding and intervening in the effects of prenatal risk factors and stressful life events; facilitating a home-school partnership; and building protective factors and facilitative processes into the educational environment.

   Transagency program development is needed in order to provide the variety of services needed by these families. These services may include

specialized medical care, family therapy, home health care, early interven-
tion services, preschool mental health services, and vocational services,
among others.

References, 26

Foreword

EXCEPTIONAL CHILDREN AT RISK
CEC Mini-Library

Many of today's pressing social problems, such as poverty, homelessness, drug abuse, and child abuse, are factors that place children and youth at risk in a variety of ways. There is a growing need for special educators to understand the risk factors that students must face and, in particular, the risks confronting children and youth who have been identified as exceptional. A child may be at risk *due to* a number of quite different phenomena, such as poverty or abuse. Therefore, the child may be at risk *for* a variety of problems, such as developmental delays; debilitating physical illnesses or psychological disorders; failing or dropping out of school; being incarcerated; or generally having an unrewarding, unproductive adulthood. Compounding the difficulties that both the child and the educator face in dealing with these risk factors is the unhappy truth that a child may have more than one risk factor, thereby multiplying his or her risk and need.

The struggle within special education to address these issues was the genesis of the 1991 CEC conference "Children on the Edge." The content for the conference strands is represented by this series of publications, which were developed through the assistance of the Division of Innovation and Development of the U.S. Office of Special Education Programs (OSEP). OSEP funds the ERIC/OSEP Special Project, a research dissemination activity of The Council for Exceptional Children. As a part of its publication program, which synthesizes and translates research in special education for a variety of audiences, the ERIC/OSEP Special Project coordinated the development of this series of books and assisted in their dissemination to special education practitioners.

Each book in the series pertains to one of the conference strands. Each provides a synthesis of the literature in its area, followed by practical suggestions—derived from the literature—for program developers, administrators, and teachers. The 11 books in the series are as follows:

- *Programming for Aggressive and Violent Students* addresses issues that educators and other professionals face in contending with episodes of violence and aggression in the schools.

- *Abuse and Neglect of Exceptional Children* examines the role of the special educator in dealing with children who are abused and neglected and those with suspected abuse and neglect.

- *Special Health Care in the School* provides a broad-based definition of the population of students with special health needs and discusses their unique educational needs.

- *Homeless and in Need of Special Education* examines the plight of the fastest growing segment of the homeless population, families with children.

- *Hidden Youth: Dropouts from Special Education* addresses the difficulties of comparing and drawing meaning from dropout data prepared by different agencies and examines the characteristics of students and schools that place students at risk for leaving school prematurely.

- *Born Substance Exposed, Educationally Vulnerable* examines what is known about the long-term effects of exposure *in utero* to alcohol and other drugs, as well as the educational implications of those effects.

- *Depression and Suicide: Special Education Students at Risk* reviews the role of school personnel in detecting signs of depression and potential suicide and in taking appropriate action, as well as the role of the school in developing and implementing treatment programs for this population.

- *Language Minority Students with Disabilities* discusses the preparation needed by schools and school personnel to meet the needs of limited-English-proficient students with disabilities.

- *Alcohol and Other Drugs: Use, Abuse, and Disabilities* addresses the issues involved in working with children and adolescents who have disabling conditions and use alcohol and other drugs.

- *Rural, Exceptional, At Risk* examines the unique difficulties of delivering education services to at-risk children and youth with exceptionalities who live in rural areas.

- *Double Jeopardy: Pregnant and Parenting Youth in Special Education* addresses the plight of pregnant teenagers and teenage parents, especially those in special education, and the role of program developers and practitioners in responding to their educational needs.

Background information applicable to the conference strand on juvenile corrections can be found in another publication, *Special Education in Juvenile Corrections*, which is a part of the CEC Mini-Library *Working with Behavioral Disorders*. That publication addresses the demographics of incarcerated youth and promising practices in responding to their needs.

1. Introduction

The media have painted a dire picture of infants who were exposed to alcohol and other drugs in utero. This picture is not fully supported by research or clinical experience with these children: We do not know the incidence of prenatal exposure to alcohol and other drugs, nor do we know the long-term effects of such exposure.

The community perception of children who have been exposed to alcohol and other drugs in utero has been shaped by print and video media coverage emphasizing the "epidemic nature" of drug abuse by pregnant women and the subsequent damage to their babies. News reports on all of the major networks have shown newborn babies who were extremely premature and/or were going through drug withdrawal.

Concern for the outcome of these children and their families underlies some major issues that currently face the field of special education. How will special education play a role in meeting their needs? What services, programs, and strategies have we developed in special education that will be helpful to these children and families who are at risk?

The incidence of substance abuse by pregnant women is not clear, nor is the incidence of substance exposure in utero. We also do not know the long-term effects of such exposure except for alcohol. The dire picture that has been painted by the media is not supported by research or clinical experience with these children. We know that the developmental outcome of children is affected not only by biological factors, but also by environmental factors such as poverty and nutrition. The services we provide to children and their families during the crucial infancy and early childhood years are also an example of an environmental factor. The nature of the services families receive and how they are provided have a major impact on outcome (Schorr & Schorr, 1988). Our hope is that education, by joining with other community agencies, can help children who are at risk due to substance exposure avoid becoming adolescents and young adults who have multiple problems such as substance abuse, dropping out of school, and juvenile delinquency.

This book reviews what we currently know about providing high-quality services to young children who have been prenatally exposed to drugs and alcohol and their families.

2. Synthesis of Research

Many women who abuse alcohol and other drugs during pregnancy also experience other psychological, social, and medical events that can affect the health of their children. Thus, the risks of substance exposure are often compounded by other difficulties, such as inadequate housing, medical care, child care, and nutrition, that place these children at risk for developmental delays.

Although this book focuses on the educational and therapeutic needs of young children who were substance exposed in utero and their families, these children often face other social realities that place them at risk for developmental difficulties. A substantial number of children in the United States today are at risk due to lack of adequate housing, medical care, nutrition, child care, and other unmet needs. For example, many of the children infected by the human immunodeficiency virus (HIV) via their mother's drug use during pregnancy are poor. They often live in inner-city areas that are affected by poverty, violence, and drug wars. Mothers may be undereducated and have few job skills; they are often single parents, dependent on Aid to Families of Dependent Children and other entitlement programs to meet their and their children's needs.

Children who were prenatally exposed to alcohol and other drugs may experience unstable living arrangements and inconsistent caregiving. They may live with different relatives or friends when they are not with their mothers, or they may be placed in foster care settings. With the increase in drug use by women of childbearing age during the 1980s has come an increase in out-of-home placement for infants and toddlers (*Conditions of Children in California*, 1989; *Ten Reasons to Invest . . .*, 1990). For example, in Los Angeles County, California, the placement of children in out-of-home residential care increased from 7.7 per 1,000 children in 1987 to 13.1 per 1,000 children in 1990; the incidence nearly doubled in less than 5 years (Children NOW, 1991).

An analysis of the impact of prenatal substance exposure must include an examination of the biological impact that drugs may have on development and learning. Such an analysis is not complete without an examination of the environmental factors that may also affect development and learning. The interrelationship of biology and environment is called an *interactionist point of view*. The developmental outcome of the child who has been prenatally exposed to drugs and alcohol will truly be the result of the interaction of biology and postnatal environment.

Biological and Medical Risk Factors

Maternal abuse of substances during pregnancy places the fetus, and later the child, at risk for a variety of medical, neurological, neuro-developmental, and behavioral difficulties (Brooks-Gunn & McCarton, 1991; Kronstadt, 1991; Zuckerman, 1991). These difficulties may become evident in utero or during delivery, or during the neonatal, infant, toddler, or preschool periods. In this section, literature will be reviewed on substance use, substance abuse and the pregnant woman, the impact of substances on the developing fetus, and the impact of substances on the developing neonate and infant.

Substance Use. Poulsen (1991) described drug marketing and drug abuse as big business in the United States. The United States is the largest importer of cocaine in the world. The Drug Enforcement Agency (DEA) estimated that we imported more than 100 metric tons in 1989 (Jehl, 1989). NIDA reported that this was a 35% increase in less than 5 years. Of the cocaine and PCP supplied in the United States, 50% and 80% respectively are supplied from California. The largest cash crop (albeit illegal) in California is marijuana. While it is particularly recognized as a problem in the large urban areas, drug use is spreading to smaller towns and rural areas.

How a drug is taken influences how quickly it reaches the brain. The form of the drug also influences how addictive it is. Generally, smokable forms are considered highly addictive and more powerful than powdered forms. For example, a social user of cocaine who "snorts" weekly may become addicted in 5 years, while a cocaine smoker may become addicted in as few as 2 weeks of daily use (Harpring, 1990). Currently the drug that is receiving the greatest attention because of its impact on the developing fetus and later on the child is crack cocaine. The primary drug of choice for given individuals varies with where they live, their ethnic/racial background, their income, and when they are being examined (Corwin, 1989; Isikoff, 1989; Ybarra & Liberman, 1989). For example, in Southern California crack is the most frequently abused illicit drug in Los Angeles County, while methamphetamine is the leader in San Diego County. Heroin is more likely to be used by Hispanic women who are addicts, while crack is more frequently used by African-American women who are addicts (Poulsen, 1991).

Most pregnant women who are addicts are users of multiple drugs, including alcohol (Burkett, Yasin, & Palow, 1990). While they may have a primary drug of choice, they abuse that drug and others depending on what is available. The seriousness of alcohol as an addictive substance must not be overlooked. In terms of documented developmental out-come on the fetus, alcohol is a known teratogen that causes fetal alcohol syndrome and fetal alcohol effects. Approximately 5% of all birth defects are associated with prenatal exposure to alcohol. Alcohol abuse is the leading cause of mental retardation in the United States (Streissguth, Sampson, & Barr, 1989).

Substance Abuse and the Pregnant Woman. Before examining the impact of substance exposure on the infant, the influence of other psychological, social, and medical events in the pregnant woman who is abusing substances must be noted. Substance abuse crosses all income levels, educational backgrounds, and racial/ethnic backgrounds. The incidence is not well established in different groups of women. One study conducted in Florida indicated that the usage rate for illicit drugs and/or alcohol ranged from 13% to 16% among pregnant women. This rate was not influenced by the socioeconomic status of the mother (Chasnoff, Landress, & Barrett, 1990). The media attention thus far has focused on women who are using publicly funded services. These mothers often have poor nutrition, impaired general health, and inadequate health care. They often do not receive regular prenatal care and may avoid the medical service system for fear of detection as addicts. They are more likely to have untreated sexually transmitted diseases and are at much greater risk for HIV infection.

The vast majority of pregnant women who are substance abusers were abused and neglected as children. Feig (1990) found that 83% had a parent who was drug or alcohol dependent, while this was the case for only 35% of nonaddicted women. Many had been sexually abused before adolescence and engaged in prostitution during adolescence to support their addiction. For example, Feig (1990) found that nearly 70% of women who were drug dependent had been sexually abused before 16 years of age, while only 15% of nonaddicted women of similar socioeconomic backgrounds had been sexually abused. As adults they are often abused and exploited by the men with whom they live. They show increased incidences of psychological problems such as clinical depression, anxiety, and suicidal ideation. They often do not complete their formal education through high school and may display learning, behavioral, and social problems. Their involvement in the drug culture often includes criminal activity such as prostitution to support their habits and may result in incarceration. Overall, these women bring a host of biological and environmental risk factors to their pregnancy in addition to substance abuse (Burkett et al., 1990; Finnegan, 1989; Griffith, 1991; Howard, Beckwith, Rodning, & Kropenske, 1989; Reed, 1987).

Not all pregnant women who are abusing drugs and alcohol match this picture. Some are functioning full time in the world of work and family. Others are attending school or completing job training programs. However, all are affected psychologically and biologically by their addiction. These effects place them and their fetuses at increased risk for developmental difficulties.

Impact of Substances on the Developing Fetus. "There is not a typical profile of the child who has been prenatally exposed to drugs and/or alcohol" (Cole, Ferrara, Johnson, Jones, Schoenbaum, Tyler, Wallace, & Poulsen, 1989; Griffith, 1991; Poulsen, 1991). Although all of the drugs discussed in this book cross the placenta and reach the fetus, their impact depends on a host of factors, such as combination of drugs used, time in pregnancy when ingested, and duration of mother's drug use. Even among women considered to be severe alcoholics who continue to drink during their entire pregnancies, 35% of the children will not display fetal alcohol syndrome (Streissguth, Sampson, & Barr, 1989).

Jones and Lopez (1988) concluded after reviewing the literature on fetal effects from maternal substance abuse that matching specific drugs with specific fetal risks was not useful. Most women are multiple drug users, and many fetal risks are common across different classes of drugs. Poulsen (1991) pointed out that the genetic resilience of the fetus, the health of the mother, her prenatal care, and the developmental status of the fetus at the time of exposure all influence what effects the substance exposure will have on the fetus and subsequently the child.

During the first trimester, substance exposure is most likely to cause structural and/or neurological damage (Briggs, 1986; Hallam, 1989; Oro & Dixon, 1987). Crack exposure causes miscarriages in up to 38% of pregnancies (Ryan, Ehrlich, & Finnegan, 1987). During the second trimester, substance exposure contributes to intrauterine failure to thrive and growth retardation (Burkett, Yasin, & Palow, 1990; Little, Snell, Klein, & Gilstrap, 1989; Smith, 1988). Being born small for gestational age places the infant at high risk for learning problems. During the third trimester, substance exposure, particularly to cocaine and heroin, may lead to premature labor and delivery (Chiang & Lee, 1985; Keith, 1989; Oro & Dixon, 1987). Prematurity is a major risk factor for developmental and learning problems.

Substance abuse can have teratogenic effects on the developing fetus (i.e., effects that cause malformation). These effects may be evident at birth or may not be manifested until later in development (Weston et al., 1989). Numerous authors have pointed to the direct effect that substance abuse has on increasing the risk of premature delivery, abruption of the placenta, spontaneous abortion, fetal distress in labor and delivery, intrauterine growth retardation, intrauterine strokes, low birth weight, sudden infant death syndrome, and sexually transmitted diseases including AIDS (see Lindenberg, Alexander, Gendrop, Nencioli, & Williams, 1991 or Kronstadt, 1991 for reviews). The teratogenic effects also may be evident through changes in structures or functions of organs and systems. For example, cocaine has a teratogenic effect on neurotransmitter function and probably indirectly affects the brain via vasocontriction (Brooks-Gunn & McCarton, 1991). Nicotine constricts maternal arteries and therefore blood flow to the uterus (Newman &

Buka, 1991). Streissguth (1990) has documented the teratogenic effects of alcohol on cardiac, renal, and facial structures. However, Zuckerman (1991) cautioned that these findings are not predictive for all infants who have been substance exposed in utero. Some infants who have been exposed do not show any clinical manifestations of such exposure. Substance exposure in utero is a *risk factor.*

The importance of prenatal care for increasing positive fetal outcome has been well documented (Griffith, 1991; Gross & Hayes, 1991; Nelson, 1990). In a 1989 study in Los Angeles County, 90% of pregnant women who were substance abusers had received minimal or no prenatal health services (Legislative Analyst, 1989). Nelson (1990) estimated that 40,000 babies in California who died shortly after birth or experienced serious medical complications would have been helped by prenatal care. Poulsen (1991) indicated from her review of the literature that the perinatal problems of women who were substance abusers and their babies would be greatly reduced by adequate prenatal care; however, she cautioned that prenatal care would not eliminate premature delivery and perinatal morbidity associated with drug use. Clearly, the impact of substance exposure interacts with the health services received by the mother during her pregnancy, even if she continues to use drugs and/or alcohol (Griffith, 1991).

Impact of Substances on the Developing Neonate and Infant. In addition to the effects of substance exposure discussed in the last section, researchers, service providers, and parents have been concerned about the possible impact of substance exposure on a child's early behavior and continuing development. Kronstadt (1991), in summarizing the research to date in this area, stated "In sum, there is little evidence that prenatal substance exposure, whether to cocaine, marijuana, opiates, tobacco or alcohol, is linked with large deficits on standardized developmental tests (p. 44)." She went on to point out, however, that much of the concern that has developed due to the dramatic increase in the number of infants who have been substance exposed has not been related to their overall performance on standardized measures of development. Rather, parents, teachers, and medical personnel are concerned about developmental sequelae believed to have an impact on how well the child interacts with his or her environment and learns from it. These are generally described as *neurobehavioral characteristics.* Many authors believe that children are most likely to show differences of delays in their development in this area (Brooks-Gunn & McCarton, 1991; Chasnoff, Griffith, MacGregor, Dirkes, & Burns, 1989; Cole et al., 1989; Griffith, 1991; Howard et al., 1989; Poulsen, 1991; Schneider & Chasnoff, 1987; Weston et al., 1989; Zuckerman, 1991). A review of the work of these authors follows.

These neurobehavioral characteristics may be apparent on early assessments of the neonate and may persist through the preschool years. The constellation of behavior is of concern because of the impact it has on how a child develops relationships with people—particularly primary caregivers—and learns from people, objects, and events in the world. Not all children who have been substance exposed will show these behaviors. Not all children who show these behaviors have been substance exposed.

As newborns, children who have been substance exposed may be more irritable and difficult to handle for feeding, bathing, and diapering. Typical caregiving activities may place the child in a state of distress and agitation. The children have been documented to have unusual acoustic characteristics to their crying, making it high pitched and piercing. When the children are agitated, they may show decreased abilities to comfort or console themselves and may not be consoled by rocking, holding, or singing. The children are also more likely to display poor feeding patterns as neonates and infants and are at increased risk for failure-to-thrive syndrome.

On neurobehavioral assessments, the neonates may display altered state regulation, disorganization, and lability. The smooth cycle from sleep to focused alertness to sleep that is seen with a typical infant may be disrupted with these babies. They may have a difficult time going to sleep and once asleep may be difficult to arouse. After awakening, they may be irritable or unresponsive to caregiver interaction. The babies may show depressed interactive abilities. Even if they are in a calm, alert state and are approached appropriately by a caregiver, they may not respond. Often they do not establish a consistent sleeping pattern and do not sleep through the night at typical ages. When awake, they may demonstrate an increased startle response and sensitivity to sounds, light, and positioning, which may make it difficult for caregivers to have positive interaction with them. These babies have been characterized as more difficult and demanding and less responsive and rewarding than even "difficult" typical babies.

Babies and infants who have been prenatally exposed to substances may display increased tremulousness and impaired motoric functioning. They may show increased muscle tone, tremors, and delays in the integration of primitive reflexes. These may combine with the previously mentioned difficulties in state regulation and generalized irritability to further complicate the child's interaction with a caregiver. The children are sometimes characterized as physically difficult to handle by caregivers.

As the babies develop, their interactions with caregivers, objects, and events in their lives continue to be influenced by the neurobehavioral risks mentioned above. The disorganization that may have characterized such an infant can continue to be manifested in the child's interactions and learning patterns. While in general development may be within normal limits, these children often continue to be at risk for social, play, emotional, and communication problems. Their "difficultness" may make it a challenge for caregivers to persist in building a consistent and nurturing relationship. Compromised capacity for state regulation may interfere with the infants' participation in sound interactive relationships with caregivers. Irritability and lability may make it difficult for them to cope with stressors in the environment. Additionally, their depressed interactive cues may be overlooked or misread by caregivers, and as a result their needs may not be met. Over all, the neurobehavioral difficulties, when they are manifested, place these children at increased risk for physical and emotional neglect and abuse by caregivers.

If an infant is displaying any of the neurobehavioral characteristics listed, the caregiver may need special support and assistance in designing an effective interactive pattern with the infant. Without such support, attachment and bonding are likely to be disrupted for both the infant and the caregiver. Without early attachment to a primary caregiver, a child's ability to develop trust, self-esteem, and positive relationships with others will be adversely affected. Such a child may be at increased risk for failure in a later educational setting, because he or she does not respond to the typical pattern of rules, routines, and reinforcers that are used to guide development and learning. Intervention geared to building a healthy bond between infant and caregiver is essential to the long-term success of these children and their families.

Psychosocial Risk Factors

Importance of the Postnatal Social Environment. Increasingly, researchers, policymakers, administrators, and direct service providers are recognizing that for children who were prenatally exposed to drugs and/or alcohol to be successful, their families must be successful. The eventual intellectual and social outcomes of children at risk are determined by both the prenatal biological risk factors and the postnatal social risk factors. Some researchers support the view that development is at least as determined by the postnatal social environment as by other factors (Bradley, 1989; Illsley, 1989; Lipsitt, 1988; Schorr & Schorr, 1988; Sigman, 1982). What do we know about the postnatal social environments in which children who were substance exposed are being raised?

The Parenting Environment. Just as there is not a typical profile with the children, there is not a typical profile with the families. Some families are intact, biological families with working parents, high incomes, and many resources. Others are living in poverty, working, and providing as many resources as they can for their children. Some children are being raised by their biological fathers. Others are being raised by single mothers who have stopped abusing drugs and are putting their lives back together. Still others are living with grandparents and extended family members. Some children are living with mothers who are still abusing drugs and/or alcohol. Others have been removed from the custody of their mothers and fathers and placed in foster care or have been adopted.

The environments in which the children are being raised are as varied as the children themselves. Most of the children who are currently being seen in early intervention programs, followed through research and intervention programs, or involved with their mothers in drug abuse treatment programs are from families who must use publicly funded services to meet their needs. Therefore, the information that follows is biased toward this sample. The picture for families who are financially able to obtain private services may be very different.

Children who were prenatally exposed to drugs and/or alcohol are often moved from placement to placement during the infant, toddler, and preschool years. For example, the preschool-aged children being served in the Los Angeles Unified School District's special pilot program for children prenatally exposed to drugs had an average of 3.1 placements each by the time they entered the program at age 3 (Cole, Jones, & Sadofsky, 1990). Even children who had only one placement still had to deal with multiple caregivers quite often, as different family members helped out or biological mothers continued to visit while the children were in foster care. Thus, these children who were at risk due to biological factors often immediately faced the postnatal social risk factors related to inconsistent caregiving, untrained caregivers, and poor attachment.

Most children spend at least some time within the biological family. This family may be living in the drug culture or in an alcohol-affected household, or, in the case of the mother who is in recovery, may still be affected by her past. An understanding of this situation is necessary for the design of effective family-centered intervention services. Woodruff and Sterzin (1991) summarized the background of families involved in their early intervention program for mothers and children with AIDS. Briefly, they pointed out that the behavior of many of the women was not consistent with building intimate, trusting relationships with service providers. They are often seen as resistant and uncooperative clients. Because of poor problem-solving and decision-making skills, their lives are often chaotic and crisis driven. Some feel that they belong in the drug culture and cannot see themselves living outside it. Because getting out will take a consistent, predictable, stable approach to decision making, they often are trapped even when their commitment to their children is such that they would like to get out. They miss appointments and do not follow through on suggestions and planned activities. Even if they discontinue their drug use, their problems with decision making and coping remain. They may display short-term memory and information processing problems. This impairs their ability to provide a stable, nurturing environment for their children. The unpredictability of the environment contributes to the children being even more difficult to handle and the mothers having more trouble making sound decisions. To be effective, intervention with these families must deal with the multiplicity of factors involved in drug abuse and the drug subculture.

Poulsen (1991) pointed out that while drug abuse crosses all socioeconomic classes, poverty, poor nutrition, educational or intellectual limitations, and/or social isolation are more frequent in mothers who are substance abusers. She outlined a number of challenges facing women who are abusing drugs and/or alcohol that are documented in the literature (Cuskey, 1982; Mondanaro, 1977; Rist, 1990; Tucker, 1979).

- Most are single parents or are with drug-using partners who offer little financial, emotional, or social support.

- Most are not financially independent. Poor minority women are 10 times more likely to be reported to child protective services than are white, middle-class substance-abusing mothers.

- Many have three or more children.

- Almost all have a history of being physically abused; many have been sexually abused as well. Many are in abusive relationships with men.

- Almost all have a history of being sexually exploited by 13 years of age.

- Many have spent time in jail for drug-related charges or prostitution, which was used to support their habit.

- A high percentage grew up in out-of-home placements or in biological families considered to be dysfunctional due to substance abuse.

- Many are lonely and socially isolated if they choose to "go clean," because their friends may remain in the drug culture.

- Many are dealing with issues of guilt, depression, separation, and loss due to the number of their children not being raised by them and the number of friends and family who have died as part of the drug culture.

- Many are experiencing difficulty becoming and remaining drug free.

- Many are naive about how children grow and develop. They have difficulty interpreting their babies' behavior;

project intentionality from birth; and think good mothers do not allow babies to mouth objects, be messy, or play with their bodies.

From *Schools Meet the Challenge: Educational Needs of Children At Risk Due to Substance Exposure* by Marie Kanne Poulsen, 1991. Sacramento: Resources in Special Education. Copyright 1991 by Resources in Special Education. Used with permission.

The quality of early infant-caregiver interactions and subsequent attachment has long-term consequences for the development of cognitive and social skills (Arend, 1979; Bell, 1970; Liberman, 1977; Matos, 1978). Mothers who are substance abusers have been found to be less attentive, responsive, and elaborative with their infants (Mondanaro, 1977; O'Connor, 1989). This behavior may result in a cycle of maternal and infant passivity that could lead to poor attachment and delays in the attainment of developmental milestones. Family-centered early intervention is necessary in order to break the cycle and ensure positive outcomes for these at-risk infant-caregiver dyads.

Children Being Raised in Foster Care. In California, Poulsen (1991) reported that more than 18,000 children under the age of 3 were residing in foster family homes, group homes, and shelters in 1989; in 1986 the number was 9,500. Up to 90% of children referred to protective services are referred for drug-related reasons. Infants who were prenatally exposed to drugs and/or alcohol tend to be placed in foster care earlier, stay longer, and have more shifts in placements. Infants who were drug exposed were still in the foster care system 5 years later.

Three of the authors of this book work in the Los Angeles area. They have seen an increase in children under age 2 being placed in group homes or group care situations. Often staff in these settings have minimal training and high turnover rates, which can contribute to poor attachment and bonding and to delays in attainment of developmental milestones. These authors have also seen foster families being pressed to take on more infants with the special needs related to drug exposure than they can handle. There are too few foster placements available (CRIC, 1990). The result is that children are moved from placement to placement during the critical infant and toddler years. Poulsen and Ambrose (1988) pointed out the importance of ensuring that a foster child has only one placement until either reunification or relinquishment occurs. Foster families, like biological families, may need added support to meet the special needs of children who have been prenatally exposed to drugs and/or alcohol. Like biological families, foster families have no typical profile.

Efforts must be directed toward supporting the parents in their parenting role, rather than removing the parents from that role (Griffith, 1991; Poulsen, 1991; Woodruff & Sterzin, 1988). The provision and coordination of these services requires a transagency, transdisciplinary effort similar to that envisioned in Part H of Public Law 99-457 (Garwood & Sheehan, 1989). The individualized family service plan (IFSP) that was proposed as the cornerstone process for service delivery in this law would be most appropriate with this population. The principle behind the IFSP is that families cannot be broken down into separate units of parent, child, grandparent and others for the purpose of service delivery. Family-centered services are essential for young children who have been prenatally exposed to drugs and their families.

Interaction of Biology and Environment

By the time the child who was substance exposed reaches preschool age, a myriad of environmental events have occurred that usually further increase the child's risk for developmental, learning, and behavioral problems. Whether the behavior that one is seeing is the impact of the drugs per se or the environment cannot usually be determined. In fact, the behavior is likely to be an interaction of the two. In terms of development, there will be a range of outcomes from this interaction (Barth, in press; Chasnoff, 1988; Griffith, 1991; Howard, Beckwith, Rodning, & Kropenske, 1989; Kronstadt, 1989; Madden, Payne, & Miller, 1986; Poulsen & Ambrose, 1990; Schnoll, 1986; Weston, Ivins, Zuckerman, Jones, & Lopez, 1989).

Children with Developmental Disabilities. Poulsen (1991) notes that of children prenatally exposed to substances, 2 to 17% will display congenital malformations at birth (Ash, 1977; Burkett et al., 1990). Some children will display mental retardation, seizure disorders, cerebral palsy, and/or physical anomalies. These children and their families will need early intervention services as defined by P.L. 99-457, Part B and Part H.

Children with Normal Development. Some children who were prenatally exposed to substances will show typical development, particularly if they are raised in stable, predictable homes with nurturing and consistent caregivers. In order to achieve this degree of consistency and nurturance, many families will require support services that have not typically been provided to children without disabilities. Estimates of the percentage of children who might show typical development if appropriate services were available to them and their families are not generally available. An investigation is being conducted by the National Association for Perinatal Addiction Research and Education (NAPARE) with 300 children who were prenatally exposed to cocaine and other drugs and/or alcohol (Griffith, 1991). The children and their families have received services beginning during pregnancy. NAPARE researchers have seen that the majority show normal patterns of development in social, emotional, and cognitive areas, with 30 to 40% showing delays in language and/or difficulties in attention. Information on these children's performance upon reaching traditional public school programs is not yet available. Whether they will be labeled as requiring special education services is not clear. Regardless of an individual child's development at a given time, the combination of biological and environmental risk factors affecting these children leads to the majority being considered at risk.

Children at Risk for Learning and Behavior Problems. The majority of children who were substance exposed in utero can be considered at risk for school failure and developmental difficulties. Again, this risk is not a result just of substance exposure, but also of environmental factors. Substance-exposed toddler and preschool-aged children have been shown to have normal intellectual abilities but less ability to modulate and control their own behavior and less task persistence than their nonexposed peers (Griffith, 1991; Howard, Beckwith, Rodning, & Kropenske, 1989; Strauss, 1981; Streissguth, 1989; Wilson, 1989). As pointed out earlier, in the NAPARE investigation approximately 30 to 40% of the substance-exposed children are showing delays in language or attentional problems. The degree of language delay or attentional problem ranges from mild articulation difficulties to severe language processing problems and from mild distractibility to diagnosed attention deficit disorder with hyperactivity. Most commonly, the children display low thresholds to overstimulation and decreased frustration tolerance.

Poulsen (1991) pointed out that *low threshold* is a term that concisely describes children who are at risk due to prenatal substance exposure. These children show uneven neurologic maturation, which is displayed through their difficulty in modulating and regulating their own behavior. This difficulty with so-called "state regulation" is present in newborns and continues to be displayed through the preschool years. When their capacities to self-regulate are overwhelmed, they may lose impulse control and display disorganized and/or inappropriate behavior. They have particular difficulty coping with transitions that are unplanned or hurried. Given the psychosocial stressors in their families' lives, such transitions are likely and contribute to high stress levels in the children. Intervention aimed at helping caregivers to provide smoother and more predictable transitions has been shown to be helpful to the children (Griffith, 1991).

These children may also deal with overstimulation and loss of self-regulation by withdrawing from the situation (Griffith, 1991; Poulsen & Ambrose, 1990). At times children who display withdrawn behavior are described as "easy babies" by their caregivers. The "easy baby" becomes a child at risk when he or she is actually underreactive, lethargic, and overly compliant. These children initiate little with caregivers, peers, or toys and materials. They are sideline observers and may miss out on the interaction necessary for typical development.

The child who is at risk due to prenatal substance exposure displays a wide range of behavioral and learning characteristics. As stated earlier, there is no typical profile of this child. However, there are some common characteristics that are helpful for practitioners and caregivers to understand as they interact with such children. These have been summarized completely by Cole, Ferrara, and colleagues (1989), and Poulsen (1991). Some children will display none of these characteristics, others only a few. Very few children will display all of the characteristics described here.

Possible behavioral characteristics include

- Exhibiting behavioral extremes.

- Becoming overstimulated easily.

- Displaying a low tolerance for changes.

- Constantly testing limits set by adults.

- Difficulty in reading social cues.

- Difficulty in establishing and maintaining relationships with peers.

Possible learning characteristics include

- Language delays.

- Sporadic mastery of skills.

- Inconsistent problem-solving strategies.

- Auditory processing and word retrieval difficulties.

- Decreased capacity to initiate and organize play.

- Decrease in focused attention and concentration.

From *Schools Meet the Challenge: Educational Needs of Children At Risk Due to Substance Exposure* by Marie Kanne Poulsen, 1991. Sacramento: Resources in Special Education. Copyright 1991 by Resources in Special Education. Used with permission.

Over all, children who have been prenatally exposed to drugs and/or alcohol show a pattern of development, beginning in infancy and continuing through the preschool years, which has led child development specialists, psychologists, pediatricians, special educators, and others to be concerned about how they will perform in the traditional public school setting. Currently, little information is available to answer questions about their success in school. More information is available on children who were prenatally exposed to alcohol than to other substances. Much information is available that points to the need to take an interactionist approach with this population and to recognize the power of environment as well as biology in their lives.

Information is beginning to be generated on the power of early intervention with these children and their families. The necessity of adopting a family-centered approach that uses resources from a variety of professional disciplines and community agencies is also being recognized (Griffith, 1991; Woodruff & Sterzin, 1988, 1990, 1991). The remaining chapters of this book provide recommendations on family-centered, transagency, transdisciplinary early intervention.

3. Implications for Practitioners

A single agency usually cannot meet all of the needs of children and families dealing with the effects of exposure to alcohol and other drugs. A family-centered system of services is needed. There are a number of things educators can do to foster the growth of these children, including understanding and intervening in the effects of prenatal risk factors and stressful life events; facilitating a home-school partnership; and building protective factors and facilitative processes into the educational environment.

Direct service providers who work on a day-to-day basis with children who were prenatally exposed to drugs and/or alcohol and their families come from a wide variety of disciplines such as nursing, special education, and vocational rehabilitation; they often work for a wide variety of agencies (e.g., hospitals, drug recovery programs, and public schools). The complex needs of the children and their families necessitate a transagency approach, because a single agency usually cannot meet all of the needs of children and families. When single agencies focus on just the needs they are able to meet, they often do not deal with the situation in a holistic manner. For example, when preschool teachers focus just on a child's behavior in the classroom, they may not develop a program that places significant emphasis on the child's past experience with multiple caregivers.

To be maximally effective, services for children and families must be transagency and transdisciplinary. Personnel from health, education, social services, children's services, drug and alcohol programs, and mental health services must work together to create a seamless system of services that are responsive to the needs of a wide variety of families. Services must be coordinated so that agencies adapt to families rather than families having to adapt to multiple agencies. Personnel from different disciplines must learn to talk a common language, preferably one that parents can understand easily. Initial referral and intake for services must be coordinated so that families need to enter the system only one time. The goal of service providers must be to make the system user friendly and supportive.

To be maximally effective, services must be family centered. Service providers must step across age boundaries and view the family as a unit, rather than separating the needs of children and their parents. Early intervention programs must empower families as major decision makers on behalf of their children. Adult treatment programs must recognize that the women they are treating are also mothers.

The family is a unit. Effective service delivery views each individual in the context of this unit. Each family unit is unique and has its own concerns and resources. A family's cultural, racial, and ethnic background has an effect on how its members interact with the service system. Service providers must increase their knowledge of cultural diversity and become more culturally competent.

Eight key elements in family-centered service delivery were identified by Shelton, Jeppson, and Johnson (1987) and have been elaborated by others (Dunst, Trivette, & Deal, 1988; Vincent, Salisbury, Strain, McCormick & Tessier, 1990; Woodruff & Sterzin, 1991). These eight elements are as follows:

- Families are the constant in children's lives, while service providers and systems come and go.

- Parent-service provider collaboration is essential at all decision-making levels.

- Complete, unbiased information about child and family care must be shared with families.

- Program policies must meet the emotional and financial needs of families.

- Family individuality and uniqueness must be respected.

- The needs of families must be incorporated into the service system, rather than the service system into the family's life.

- Parent-to-parent and family-to-family support must be facilitated.

- Service delivery systems must be responsive to family needs and be flexible and accessible.

In a family-centered system of services, families are viewed as competent identifiers of their concerns and priorities. The task of service providers is to help them in this identification process and then to help identify resources that the families will find acceptable to meet their priorities. Families are the decision makers for themselves and their children. Parents' opinions about a child's development and needs are considered just as important as professional opinion. Building a relationship with the family based on respect for a family's uniqueness and capabilities should be a major goal of the service provider.

Implications for Educational Personnel

Educational personnel include teachers, school psychologists, teaching assistants, speech and language therapists or clinicians, and adaptive physical educators. The majority of the recommendations presented here have grown out the work of the Los Angeles Unified School District's program for preschool age children prenatally exposed to drugs (Cole, Ferrara et al., 1989; Cole, Jones, & Sadofsky, 1990). Program personnel have identified basic assumptions for personnel working with the children and protective factors and facilitative processes to be built into classrooms for young children prenatally exposed to drugs and/or alcohol.

Basic Assumptions. Ten assumptions that should guide the development of educational services for these young children have been identified by Cole, Ferrara, and colleagues (1989). These are as follows:

- Facilitating a home-school partnership is an essential part of the curriculum.

- Each child and family must be served as individuals with particular strengths and vulnerabilities; attempting to list common characteristics for both children and mothers hides the unique strengths and vulnerabilities of each mother-child relationship.

- These children are more like than different from their typical peers.

- Prenatal drug exposure can cause a continuum of impairments from severe disabling conditions to risk factors; however there is no "typical profile."

- Children show a pattern of performance that is often inconsistent and unpredictable; they master skills sporadically.

- Behaviors are the result of a constellation of risk factors resulting from possible organic damage, early insecure attachment patterns, and often ongoing environmental instability.

- Intervention strategies, to be effective, must attempt to counteract prenatal risk factors and stressful life events; protective factors and facilitative processes must be built into classrooms.

- Better coping skills require increased self-esteem, self-control, and problem-solving mastery.

- Program intervention is best achieved when all professionals concerned with the family have regularly scheduled times to meet and plan.

- Research has shown that the progress of children at risk is enhanced when they are placed in predictable, secure, and stable environments where they can form attachments with nurturing, caring adults such as teachers and baby-sitters.

In order to work effectively with young children prenatally exposed to drugs and/or alcohol in the toddler or preschool classroom setting, educators must recognize the vulnerabilities of the children—vulnerabilities that come from both biological and environmental risk factors. Educators must also recognize the children's strengths and the ways in which they are like typical children. When the children display difficulties in development, learning, or behavior, appropriate intervention strategies must be selected. These strategies come from years of providing services to young at-risk children and children with developmental disabilities.

In the opinion of the authors, children who were prenatally exposed to drugs and/or alcohol do not need a separate curriculum or teaching methodology; they need systematic application of what we know about successful early intervention (Bredekamp, 1986; McCracken, 1986; Strain, 1990; Vincent et al., 1990). The educational personnel from the Los Angeles Unified School District program have done this through their development of a document entitled *Today's Challenge: Teaching Strategies for Working with Young Children Pre-natally Exposed to Drugs/Alcohol* (Cole, Ferrara et al., 1989). They divide the strategies into two areas: protective classroom factors and facilitative classroom processes.

Protective Factors to Be Built into a Classroom.

- Curriculum: Curricula should be developmentally appropriate and promote experiential learning—interaction, exploration, and play in a context that is interesting and relevant.

- Play: Adults must actively facilitate children's play activities by helping them extend the complexity and duration of such activities.

- Routines and rituals: Children need a setting that is predictable; continuity and reliability should be provided through routines and rituals.

- Rules: The setting should be one in which the number of rules specifically told to the children is limited.

- Observation and assessment: Assessments should be made during play, at transition time, and while the child is engaged in self-help activities.

- Flexible room environment: The setting should allow materials and equipment to be removed to reduce stimuli or added to enrich the activity.

- Transition time plans: Transition should be seen as an activity in and of itself with a beginning, middle, and end.

- Adult/child ratio: There should be enough adults to promote attachment, predictability, nurturing and ongoing assistance in learning appropriate coping styles.

These protective factors focus on planning that educational personnel can do before they bring children into a classroom setting. They are general guidelines for the design of toddler and preschool environments for all children. The assumption is not that young children who were prenatally exposed to drugs and/or alcohol will be placed in separate classrooms. The experience of the Los Angeles Unified School District is that a majority of the children can be served in the toddler or preschool settings where their typical peers are receiving service.

Facilitative Processes to Be Built into a Classroom.

- Attachment: A major goal for each child is to develop an attachment to one of the adults in the classroom.

- Respect: Adults must respect children's work and play space.

- Feelings: Feelings are important and legitimate; there is a reason for children's actions and behavior even though adults may not be able to figure it out.

- Mutual discussion: Talking about behavior and feelings validates the child's experiences and sets up an accepting atmosphere. Adults should respond with empathy, not judgment.

- Role model: Teachers need to model behavior that is appropriate for children to imitate.

- Peer sensitivity: Until children have the experience of having their own needs met repeatedly and consistently, they will not become aware of the needs and feelings of others.

- Decision making: Teachers need to recognize the importance of allowing children to make decisions for themselves and provide many opportunities for such decision making.

- Home-school partnership: Establishing a close working relationship with the home is an essential part of the curriculum, strengthening the positive interaction between child and family and increasing parental confidence and competency.

- Transdisciplinary model: The activities of all professionals concerned with the child and family should be coordinated.

The strategies identified as facilitative processes shape educational personnel's interaction with children and families on a daily basis. They are designed to counteract or help children cope with stressful life events they may be experiencing. In addition, the strategies are designed to provide children support in coping with any neurodevelopmental behaviors that may impede their learning and classroom performance. These strategies can be combined with teaching techniques of using play as a learning activity and providing individualized and small-group guidance to assist children in mastering new skills. Most children who are experiencing difficulties in self-regulation and behavior modulation do give early warning signals (e.g., increased rates of behavior or randomness of activities) that can serve as a cue that they are losing control. Learning the cues for individual children is essential. This is often a good starting point for interacting with families and reinforcing the concept that they do know their own children. Often parents are well aware of these behavioral cues.

The focus must be on the child's social environment as well as prenatal exposure to drugs and/or alcohol. As educators, we cannot change the prenatal exposure, but we can give children support and new skills for dealing with the world in which they live. If we form a cooperative partnership with their families and other community agencies, we can work to change the social situation in which they live. We can be effective in helping children and families function in the educational mainstream.

Over all, these assumptions and protective factors and facilitative processes point to the findings from the research literature presented in Chapter 2. We do not know what the outcome for individual children and families will be simply because of prenatal exposure to drugs and/or alcohol. Outcome is dependent on the interaction of biological and environmental events. One powerful set of environmental events is the intervention services that we choose to offer to these children and families. Services that are comprehensive, coordinated, transagency, and transdisciplinary, if they are delivered from a family-centered perspective, can support these children and families in achieving success in the mainstream of our educational and community settings.

4. Implications for Program Development and Administration

Transagency program development is needed in order to provide the variety of services needed by these families. These services may include specialized medical care, family therapy, home health care, early intervention services, preschool mental health services, and vocational services, among others.

To provide a perspective on program development activities, we have developed the following list of services that the young children who were prenatally exposed to substances and their families used in our various programs. These services were not provided by one agency and, in terms of the audience for this book, are not assumed to be the responsibility of public education on its own. The list points to the need for transagency program development and administration. Needed services include

- Specialized medical care for the child dealing with the effects of drug exposure and HIV infection and for other infected family members, preferably at the same facility and at the same time.

- Family therapy aimed at developing healthy, functional relationships among family members.

- Adequate chemical dependency recovery programs for mothers that allow them to keep their children with them during recovery.

- Babysitting and respite care services.

- Prenatal care, including nutrition counseling and food.

- Home health care and homemaker services.

- Parent-infant interaction programs.

- Early intervention services for children who are showing developmental difficulties.

- Preschool services for children that support their learning and development even if they are not showing delays.
- Mental health services and emotional support for families, including parent-to-parent and professional-to-parent services.
- Family stress management instruction.
- Information and assistance in obtaining safe and affordable housing.
- High school completion and vocational instruction.
- Assistance in obtaining a job.
- Transportation planning and assistance.
- Specialized foster care for children and/or mother-child pairs when the biological family is unable to care for them.
- Adoption services when family members are unable to care for the child who has been substance exposed.
- A 24-hour information and crisis support hotline.
- Stipends to extended family members caring for children.
- Health and social services for undocumented aliens who are parents of children who are substance exposed.
- Life skills instruction.
- Clothing for children and adults.
- Food and basic household supplies.

Many other services could be added to this list depending on where a family lives, how many children are in the family, and how healthy the children are. The major task of program developers and administrators is to network with other private and public providers in the community. Woodruff and Sterzin (1991) summarized the recommendations of Schorr and Schorr (1988) as follows:

> In order to succeed with families with multiple needs, programs must offer "a broad spectrum of services," must "cross traditional professional and bureaucratic boundaries," must be "flexible," must "see the child in the context of family and the family in the context of its surroundings," must be offered by "people who care about them and respect them, people they can trust," must offer services that are "coherent and easy to use," must offer "continuity of services from a small, committed team," must find ways to "adapt to or circum-

vent traditional professional and bureaucratic limitations when necessary to meet the needs of those they serve," and must be offered by "professionals who are able to redefine their roles" to respond to needs. (pp. 257–259)

Services to women who are drug dependent must focus on their recovery, their life skills, and, in the case of women with children, their parenting skills. Services to children who were prenatally exposed to drugs and/or alcohol must focus on their biological and environmental risk factors. They must counteract negative life events that children are experiencing. For both mothers and children, services must focus on increasing coping and problem solving skills. In order to provide these types of services, communities will have to build transagency models of planning and service delivery.

Experts in the drug recovery and child welfare fields believe that programs must "support the mother, protect the infant and promote positive mother-infant interaction and formation of a positive relationship" (Weston et al., 1989, p. 6). Lief (1985) suggested that such comprehensive services would help these mothers "unravel the strands of disorder and make possible a reasonably constructive design for living" (p. 74). To be most effective for parents and children, services must help both achieve their maximum potential.

Transagency/transdisciplinary service delivery requires a commitment to community consensus building and the involvement of direct service personnel in interagency planning and program development. It also requires viewing families as equals in the decision-making process. Both of these commitments will mean additional training for existing staff members who are generally trained to operate within the confines of their own program. In the case of educational personnel, this often translates to the confines of their own classroom. Administrators must provide leadership in this process of community collaboration and support the involvement of their staff, including training in consensus building and shared decision making with families. The area of families as competent decision makers needs particularly careful attention.

The general media image of children prenatally exposed to drugs and/or alcohol has not been a hopeful one. The children are portrayed as "marked" for life. The image painted of their families is equally bleak: They are shown as uncaring and uncommitted. Our experience over the last 4 or 5 years as we have worked with these children and families does not support either image. Neither the research nor model program literature supports this image. We must begin to confront the bigotry inherent in this negative view. Educational personnel need information on the diversity of family values and forms and the capability of families to act positively on behalf of their children. The model projects presented at the workshop upon which this book is based support a more hopeful view for both children and families. Such a view is realistic if we build family-centered, community-based, coordinated, transagency services.

These services must be joined with services for other young children and families. The danger of labeling, stereotyping, and segregating children because of maternal substance abuse cannot be overemphasized. Not every child who demonstrates some of the behavior discussed in this book was prenatally exposed to drugs and/or alcohol. Many other risk factors also result in learning, behavioral, and developmental problems. Not every child who was prenatally exposed to drugs and/or alcohol will show problems in development, learning or behavior. Children who were prenatally exposed to substances are unique, but as a whole they are more like than different from other children. The environmental risk factors they face seem to be at least as critical as their biological risk factors in determining their developmental outcome. The label *prenatally exposed to drugs and/or alcohol* does not mean that one teaching strategy will be more effective than another or that one curriculum should be used over another or that one staffing pattern is needed over another. There is a danger in this label in that it can engender a self-fulfilling prophecy: Children will become what their parents and teachers expect them to become. Given the current view of drug exposure this would be an unfair prophecy. There is also a danger in labeling the parents. Alcohol and drug addiction is an illness, not a moral shortcoming. Labeling mothers as having exposed their children when very little treatment is currently available to those with this illness is mean-spirited, if not unethical. Also, such labeling implies that the parent is not interested in the child; this does not match the experience of these authors over the past 4 or 5 years.

Schorr and Schorr (1988) identified the following six steps necessary for implementing services that work for families.

1. *Knowing what works.* We now have the beginning of a data base on what works, that is, family-centered, comprehensive, coordinated, transagency, community-based care.

2. *Proving we can afford it.* The alternative to affording such forward-looking services when children are young is to pay later in high school dropout, teenage alcohol and drug abuse, teen pregnancy, juvenile delinquency, out-of-home placement, and so forth.

3. *Attracting and training enough skilled and committed personnel.* This new vision of service delivery will require staff development in all of the major agencies that now interact with children and families. Of particular concern is the recruiting of individuals from the diverse cultures served by these agencies. Currently, there is a shortage of qualified personnel from minority groups in the human service fields (Federal Bureau of Labor Statistics, 1988). The poten-

tial role of experienced parents with new parents entering the system needs to be explored further.

The last three steps have to do with replicating model programs once they have been developed or identified:

4. *Resisting the lure of replication through dilution.*

5. *Gentling the heavy hand of bureaucracy.*

6. *Devising a variety of replication strategies.*

These steps will require administrative leadership and support for doing what we know has made a difference, rather than just doing a piece of it here and a piece of it there. The continued community coordination of services coupled with a family-centered approach to service delivery should help to gentle the bureaucracy. If the model proposed in P.L. 99-457, Part H, for children from birth to 3 years of age and their families is fully implemented, we will be well on our way to having families expect that they will be treated with respect. The individualized family service plan (IFSP) that is the cornerstone of this family-centered service delivery model clearly places parents in the role of taking on as much decision making as they like on behalf of their children.

There will be a need for long-term model adaptation of what is learned through P.L. 99-457 and the many community-based projects being funded in different areas of the country and for different populations through departments of health and social services and drug and alcohol programs. We have the beginning of an answer. Now we must continue to explore and expand with new populations and communities. The early picture that was painted in the popular press and media was inaccurate. The children and families described here have capabilities as well as vulnerabilities. They are first and foremost individuals in need of services that meet their concerns. We have the opportunity to build a partnership with them, a partnership that is focused on a successful future. We will not be able to do it with education services alone or health services alone; we must build transagency models of comprehensive, coordinated service delivery and we must start when the children are very young—before birth with prenatal care and after birth with a wide range of child and family support services.

References

Arend, R. (1979). Continuity of individual application from infancy to kindergarten. *Child Development, 50,* 950–959.

Ash, P. (1977). The incidence of hereditary disease in man. *Lancet, 1,* 849–851.

Barth R. (In press). Educational implications of prenatally drug exposed children. *Social Work in Education.*

Bell, S. (1970). The development of the concept of object as related to infant-mother attachment. *Child Development, 41,* 291–311.

Bradley, R. (1989). Home environment and cognitive development in the first year of life. *Developmental Psychology, 25,* 217–235.

Bredekamp, S. (Ed.). (1986). *Developmentally appropriate practice.* Washington, DC: NAEYC.

Briggs, G., (1986). *Drugs in pregnancy and lactation.* Baltimore, MD: Williams and Wilkins.

Brooks-Gunn, J., & McCarton, C. (1991). *Effects of drugs in-utero on infant development.* National Institute of Child Health and Human Development, Report to Congress.

Burkett, G., Yasin, S., & Palow, D. (1990). Perinatal implication of cocaine exposure. *Journal of Reproductive Medicine, 35*(1), 35–42.

Chasnoff, I. (1988). *A first national hospital incidence study.* Chicago: National Association for Perinatal Addiction Research and Education.

Chasnoff, I., Griffith, D., MacGregor, S., Dirkes, K., & Burns, K. (1989). Temporal patterns of cocaine use in pregnancy: Perinatal outcome. *Journal of the American Medical Association, 261,* 12, 1741–1744.

Chasnoff, I. Landress, H., & Barrett, M. (1990). The prevalence of illicit drug and or alcohol use during pregnancy and discrepancies in mandatory reporting in Pinellas County, Florida. *New England Journal of Medicine, 322,* 1202–1206.

Chiang, C., & Lee, C. (Eds.) (1985). *Prenatal drug exposure: Kinetics and dynamics.* Rockville, MD: National Institute on Drug Abuse.

Children NOW. *California: The state of our children 1991.* Santa Monica, CA: Author.

Cole, C., Ferrara, V., Johnson, D., Jones, M., Schoenbaum, M., Tyler, R., Wallace, V., & Poulsen, M. (1989). *Today's challenge: Teaching strategies for working with young children pre-natally exposed to drugs/alcohol.* Los Angeles, CA: Los Angeles Unified School District.

Cole, C., Jones, M., & Sadofsky, G. (1990). Working with children at risk due to prenatal substance exposure. *PRISE Reporter, 21*, 5.

Conditions of children in California (1989). Berkeley: Policy Analysis for California Education (PACE), School of Education, University of California.

Corwin, M. (1989, October). Patent form of speed could be drug of 90's. *Los Angeles Times.*

CRIC (Children's Research Institute of California). (1990). *A report on the foster children's health project of San Diego County.* Sacramento, CA: Author.

Cuskey, W. (1982). Female addictions: A review of the literature. *Journal of Addictions and Health, 3*, 3–33.

Dunst, C., Trivette, C., & Deal, A. (1988). *Enabling and empowering families: Principles and guidelines for practice.* Cambridge, MA: Brookline Books.

Federal Bureau of Labor Statistics. (1988). *Occupational Outlook Handbook.* Washington, DC: U.S. Government Printing Office.

Feig, L. (1990). *Drug exposed infants and children: Service needs and policy questions.* Washington, DC: Department of Health and Human Services.

Finnegan, L. (1989). *Drug dependency in pregnancy: Clinical management of mother and child.* Washington, DC: National Institute of Drug Abuse Service Research Monograph Service, U.S. Government Printing Office.

Garwood, G., & Sheehan, R. (1989). *Designing a comprehensive early intervention system: The challenge of PL 99-457.* Austin, TX: Pro-Ed.

Griffith, D. (1991, May). *Intervention needs of children prenatally exposed to drugs.* Congressional testimony before the House Select Committee on Special Education.

Gross, R., & Hayes, C. (1991). Implementing a multisite multidisciplinary clinical trial: The infant health and development program. *Zero to Three, 11*(4), 1–7.

Hallam, H. (1989). Medical controversies in evaluation and management of cocaine exposed infants. In *Special currents: Cocaine babies.* Columbus, OH: Ross Laboratories.

Harpring, J. (Ed.). (1990). *Cocaine babies: Florida's substance exposed youth.* Tallahassee: Florida Department of Education.

Howard, J., Beckwith, L., Rodning, C., & Kropenske, V. (1989, June). The development of young children of substance abusing parents: Insights from seven years of intervention and research. *Zero to Three,* pp. 8–12.

Illsley, R., (1989). *Low birth weight: A medical, psychological and social study.* New York: Wiley.

Isikoff, M. (1989, Februray 19). In rural America crank, not crack, is drug plague. *Los Angeles Times.*

Jehl, D. (1989, April 13). Popularity of crack fuels cocaine boom. *Los Angeles Times.*

Jones, C., & Lopez, R. (1988). *Direct and indirect effects on infant of maternal drug use.* Rockville, MD: NIDA.

Keith, L. (1989). Substance abuse in pregnant women: Recent experiences at the perinatal center for chemical dependence of Northwestern Memorial Hospital. *Obstetrics and Gynecology, 73,* 5.

Kronstadt, D. (1989). *Pregnancy and cocaine addiction: An overview of impact and treatment.* San Francisco, CA: Far West Laboratory for Educational Research and Development.

Kronstadt, D. (1991). Complex developmental issues of prenatal drug exposure. *The Future of Children, 1*(1), 36–49.

Legislative Analyst (1989). Substance exposed infants. *The 1989–1990 budget: Perspectives and issues.* Report to the California Joint Legislative Budget Committee, Sacramento, CA.

Liberman, A. (1977). Preschooler's competence with a peer: Relation with attachment and peer experience. *Child Development, 48,* 1277–1287.

Lief, P. (1985). The drug user as a parent. *The International Journal of the Addictions, 20*(1), 63–97.

Lindenberg, C., Alexander, E., Gendrop, S., Nencioli, M., & Williams, D. (1991). A review of the literature on cocaine abuse in pregnancy. *Nursing Research, 40*(2), 69–75.

Lipsitt, L. (1988). Infant mental health: Enigma or brilliant breakthrough. *Child Behavior and Development Letter, 7,* 9.

Little, B., Snell, L., Klein, V., & Gilstrap, L. (1989). Cocaine abuse complicates pregnancy. *Obstetrics and Gynecology, 73,* 151–160.

Madden, J., Payne, T., & Miller, S. (1986). Maternal cocaine use and effects on the newborn. *Pediatrics, 77,* 209–211.

Matos, L., (1978). Continuity and adaptation in the second year: The relationship between quality of attachment and later competence. *Child Development, 49,* 549–556.

McCracken, J. (Ed.). (1986). *Reducing stress in young children's lives.* Washington, DC: NAEYC.

Mondanaro, J. (1977). Women: Pregnancy, children and addiction. *Journal of Psychedelic Drugs, 9,* 1.

Nelson, H. (1990, February 3) Priced out of prenatal care: Infant mortality up. *Los Angeles Times.*

Newman, L., & Buka, S. (1991, Spring). Clipped wings. *American Educator*, pp. 27–34.

O'Connor, M. (1989, April). *The influence of mother-child interaction on behavioral outcome of infants exposed to alcohol prenatally*. Paper presented at The Society for Research in Child Development, Kansas City, Missouri.

Oro, A., & Dixon, S. (1987). Fetal and neonatal medicine: Perinatal cocaine and methamphetamine exposure. *Journal of Pediatrics, 111*, 571–578.

Poulsen, M., & Ambrose, S. (1988). *Child develpment issues and implications for shelter care*. Sacramento: Children's Research Institute of California.

Poulsen M. (1991). *Schools meet the challenge: Educational needs of children at risk due to substance exposure*. Sacramento: Resources in Special Education.

Reed, B. (1987). Developing women sensitive drug dependent treatment services: Why so difficult? *Journal of Psychoactive Drugs*, 151–164.

Rist, M. (1990, January). The shadow children. *The American School Board Journal*, pp. 19–24.

Ryan, L., Ehrlich, S., & Finnegan, L. (1987). Cocaine abuse in pregnancy: Effects in the fetus and newborn. *Neurotoxicology and Tetralogy, 9*, 295–299.

Schneider, J., & Chasnoff, I. (1987). Cocaine abuse during pregnancy: Its effects on infant motor development—A clinical perspective. *Topics in Acute Care Trauma Rehabilitation, 2*(1), 59–69.

Schnoll, S. (1986). Pharmacological bases of perinatal addiction. In I. Chasnoff (Ed.), *Drug use in pregnancy* (pp. 27–52). Boston: MTP Press.

Schorr, L., & Schorr, D. (1988). *Within our reach*. New York: Doubleday.

Shelton, T., Jeppson, E., & Johnson, B. (1987). *Family-centered care for children with special health care needs*. Washington, DC: Association for the Care of Children's Health.

Sigman, M. (1982). Plasticity in development: Implications for intervention. In L. Bond & J. Jaffee (Eds.), *Facilitating infants and early childhood development* (pp. 117–152). Hanover, NH: University of New England Press.

Smith, J. (1988). The danger of prenatal cocaine use. *Maternal Child Nursing, 13*, 174–179.

Strain, P. (1990). LRE for preschool children with handicaps: What we know, what we should be doing. *Journal of Early Intervention, 14*(4), 291–296.

Strauss, A. (1981). Neonatal manifestations of maternal phencyclidine (PCP) abuse. *Pediatrics, 66*, 4.

Streissguth, A. (1989, April). *Prenatal alcohol exposure and child IQ, achievement and classroom behavior at age 7*. Paper presented at the Society for Research in Child Development, Kansas City, MO.

Streissguth, A. (1990). Fetal alcohol syndrome and the teratogenicity of alcohol. *The Bulletin of the King's County Medical Society, 69*, 5.

Streissguth, A., Sampson, P., & Barr, H. (1989). Neurobehavioral dose-response effects of prenatal alcohol exposure in human from infancy to adulthood. In D. Hutchings (Ed.), *Prenatal abuse of licit and illicit drugs. Annals of The New York Academy of Sciences, 562*.

Ten reasons to invest in the families of California (1990). Prepared and published by County Welfare Directors Association of California, Chief Probation Officers Association of California and California Mental Health Directors Association.

Tucker, M. (1979). A descriptive and comparative analysis of the social support structure of heroin addicted women. In *Addicted women: Family dynamics, self perception and support systems*. Washington, DC: NIDA, U.S. Government Printing Office.

Vincent, L., Salisbury, C., Strain, P., McCormick, C., & Tessier, A. (1990). A behavioral-ecological approach to early intervention: Focus on cultural diversity. In S. Meisels & J. Shonkoff (Eds.), *Handbook of early intervention* (pp. 173–195). Cambridge: Cambridge University Press.

Weston, D., Ivins, B., Zuckerman, B., Jones, C., & Lopez, R. (1989). Drug-exposed babies: Research and clinical issues. *Zero to Three, 9*(5), 1–7.

Wilson, G. (1989). Clinical studies of infants and children exposed prenatally to heroin. *Annals of The New York Academy of Sciences, 562*, 183–194.

Woodruff, G., & Sterzin, E. (1988, May–June). The transagency approach: A model for serving children with HIV infection and their families. *Children Today*, pp. 9–14.

Woodruff, G., & Sterzin, E. (1990). Working with drug-dependent parents and children at risk for HIV infection: A community-based model of service delivery. In G. Anderson (Ed.), *Courage to care: Responding to the crisis of children with AIDS* (pp. 191–210). Washington, DC: Child Welfare League of America.

Woodruff, G., & Sterzin, E. (1991). *Family support services for drug and AIDS affected families*. Unpublished manuscript.

Ybarra, M., & Liberman, P. (1989, August 4). U.S. labels Los Angeles a center of drug trade, violence. *Los Angeles Times*.

Zuckerman, B. (1991). Drug-exposed infants: Understanding the medical risk. *The Future of Children, 1*(1), 26–35.

CEC Mini-Library
Exceptional Children at Risk

A set of 11 books that provide practical strategies and interventions for children at risk.

- *Programming for Aggressive and Violent Students.* Richard L. Simpson, Brenda Smith Miles, Brenda L. Walker, Christina K. Ormsbee, & Joyce Anderson Downing. No. P350. 1991. 42 pages.

- *Abuse and Neglect of Exceptional Children.* Cynthia L. Warger with Stephanna Tewey & Marjorie Megivern. No. P351. 1991. 44 pages.

- *Special Health Care in the School.* Terry Heintz Caldwell, Barbara Sirvis, Ann Witt Todaro, & Debbie S. Accouloumre. No. P352. 1991. 56 pages.

- *Homeless and in Need of Special Education.* L. Juane Heflin & Kathryn Rudy. No. P353. 1991. 46 pages.

- *Hidden Youth: Dropouts from Special Education.* Donald L. Macmillan. No. P354. 1991. 37 pages.

- *Born Substance Exposed, Educationally Vulnerable.* Lisbeth J. Vincent, Marie Kanne Poulsen, Carol K. Cole, Geneva Woodruff, & Dan R. Griffith. No. P355. 1991. 30 pages.

- *Depression and Suicide: Special Education Students at Risk.* Eleanor C. Guetzloe. No. P356. 1991. 45 pages.

- *Language Minority Students with Disabilities.* Leonard M. Baca & Estella Almanza. No P357. 1991. 56 pages.

- *Alcohol and Other Drugs: Use, Abuse, and Disabilities.* Peter E. Leone. No. P358. 1991. 33 pages.

- *Rural, Exceptional, At Risk.* Doris Helge. No. P359. 1991. 48 pages.

- *Double Jeopardy: Pregnant and Parenting Youth in Special Education.* Lynne Muccigrosso, Marylou Scavarda, Ronda Simpson-Brown, & Barbara E. Thalacker. No. P360. 1991. 44 pages.

Save 10% by ordering the entire library, No. P361, 1991. Call for the most current price information, 703/620-3660.

Send orders to:
The Council for Exceptional Children, Dept. K11150
1920 Association Drive, Reston VA 22091-1589